TAKE IT EASY, CHARLIE BROWN

by Charles M. Schulz

Selected Cartoons from
You'll Flip, Charlie Brown, Vol. 2

A FAWCETT CREST BOOK

Fawcett Publications, Inc., Greenwich, Conn.

Other Peanuts Books in Fawcett Crest Editions
Include the Following:

YOU'RE A PAL, SNOOPY! D1638
  (selected cartoons from You Need Help,
  Charlie Brown, Vol. 2)

WHAT NOW, CHARLIE BROWN? D1699
  (selected cartoons from The Unsinkable
  Charlie Brown, Vol. 1)

YOU'RE SOMETHING SPECIAL, SNOOPY D1722
  (selected cartoons from The Unsinkable
  Charlie Brown, Vol. 2)

YOU'VE GOT A FRIEND, CHARLIE BROWN D1754
  (selected cartoons from You'll Flip,
  Charlie Brown, Vol. 1)

Only 50¢ Each—Wherever Paperbacks Are Sold

If your bookdealer is sold out, send cover price plus 15¢ each for postage and handling to Mail Order Department, Fawcett Publications, Inc., Greenwich, Connecticut 06830. Please order by number and title. Orders accepted only for the U.S. and possessions. Catalog available on request.

TAKE IT EASY, CHARLIE BROWN

This book, prepared especially for Fawcett Publications, Inc., comprises the second half of YOU'LL FLIP, CHARLIE BROWN, and is reprinted by arrangement with Holt, Rinehart & Winston, Inc.

Copyright © 1965, 1966, 1967 by United Feature Syndicate, Inc.

Printed in the United States of America
February 1973

➤

CLOMP!

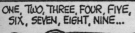

YOU'VE BEEN USING MY TOOTHBRUSH!

→

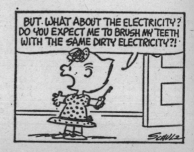

MIGHT AS WELL TURN THIS OFF..
THERE'S NO ONE WATCHING IT...

CLICK

NO ONE
WATCHING IT?

WADDYA MEAN, NO
ONE? I'M SOMEONE!

MY MOTHER IS ALWAYS COMPLAINING ABOUT HAVING TO MAKE LUNCHES

WHAT'S SO HARD ABOUT IT? THIS MORNING I TOLD HER I'D MAKE MY OWN LUNCH

AND I DID, TOO! SEE? I MADE MY OWN LUNCH..

EIGHT CANDY BARS!

A MEASLES SHOT... GOOD GRIEF!

WHY GET VACCINATED? WHY NOT JUST WEAR SOMETHING RED OR DRINK SOME ELDERBERRY BLOSSOM TEA?

THOSE ARE OLD WIVES' CURES

SOME OF THOSE OLD WIVES WERE PRETTY SHARP!

WHAT'S THIS BOARD FOR?

THAT'S NOT A BOARD.. THAT'S A TRAP DOOR

IF YOU LIFT THAT TRAP DOOR, YOU'LL FIND A LONG STAIRWAY GOING DOWN FOURTEEN FLIGHTS AND LEADING TO HUGE STOREROOMS FILLED WITH TOYS AND ALL SORTS OF CANDY...

YOU'RE PUTTING ME ON!

TODAY THE NEIGHBORHOOD, TOMORROW THE WORLD!

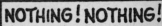

LADIES AND GENTLEMEN, THE LINEUPS FOR TODAY'S GAME...

INDULGING IN A LITTLE FANTASY, EH, CHARLIE BROWN? OKAY, LET'S PRETEND I'M THE CATCHER...

ALL RIGHT, PITCHER...WE'VE GOT TO GET OUR SIGNALS STRAIGHT....ONE FINGER WILL MEAN A FAST BALL, TWO FINGERS WILL MEAN A CURVE AND YOU KNOW WHAT THREE FINGERS WILL MEAN?

THREE FINGERS WILL MEAN A SNOWBALL! HA! HA! HA! HA! HA!

HER KIND KNOWS NO SEASON!

SCHULZ

GOOD GRIEF! IT SNOWED LAST NIGHT!

SO HERE I. AM COVERED BY A SOFT BLANKET OF SNOW... I THINK I'LL LEAP UP AND SCATTER IT IN ALL DIRECTIONS...

OKAY, LINUS, TELL ME ALL ABOUT THE "GREAT PUMPKIN"

WELL, IT'S LIKE THIS...

ON HALLOWEEN NIGHT, THE "GREAT PUMPKIN" CHOOSES THE PUMPKIN PATCH THAT HE THINKS IS THE MOST SINCERE... THEN HE RISES OUT OF THE PUMPKIN PATCH, AND FLIES THROUGH THE AIR BRINGING PRESENTS TO CHILDREN EVERYWHERE

I BELIEVE YOU!

YOU DO?!

FANTASTIC!

SCHULZ

SCHULZ

HELLO?

HELLO, LUCILLE? YOUR KID BROTHER JUST LEFT HERE A FEW MINUTES AGO...MAYBE YOU CAN WATCH FOR HIM SO HE DOESN'T GET LOST... YEAH...HE AND THAT FUNNY LOOKING KID WITH THE BIG NOSE

YEAH, HE TOLD ME THAT WHOLE RIDICULOUS AND IMPOSSIBLE STORY ABOUT THE "GREAT PUMPKIN"... THAT'S THE WILDEST STORY I'VE EVER HEARD...

BUT I BELIEVE IT!!

HELLO, LINUS? I HAVE A PROBLEM...YEAH, IT'S ME.. PEPPERMINT PATTY...

NOW, YOU TOLD ME THAT THE "GREAT PUMPKIN" WOULD APPEAR IF I HAD A VERY SINCERE PUMPKIN PATCH...NOW, YOU ALSO KNOW THAT I DIDN'T HAVE A PUMPKIN PATCH..

WELL, I WENT OUT AND BOUGHT TEN PUMPKINS, AND TRIED TO FAKE, IF YOU'LL PARDON THE EXPRESSION, A PUMPKIN PATCH...NOW, YOU TELL ME, AND TELL ME STRAIGHT...AM I A **HYPOCRITE**?!!

WHAT DO I TELL HER?

DON'T ASK ME.. YOU'RE THE THEOLOGIAN!

SCHULZ

COULD I HAVE AN EXTRA APPLE, PLEASE, FOR MY BLOCKHEAD BROTHER? HE'S SITTING IN A PUMPKIN PATCH TONIGHT....HE'S SORT OF WAITING...

WHAT IS HE WAITING FOR? HE'S WAITING FOR THE "GREAT PUMPKIN" TO APPEAR...THAT'S RIGHT.. COULD I HAVE THE EXTRA APPLE? THANK YOU...

OH, BROTHER!

TRICKS OR TREATS..

COULD I HAVE AN EXTRA CUP CAKE FOR MY NUTTY BROTHER, PLEASE? HE'S NOT WITH ME...

HE COULDN'T COME...HE'S SITTING IN A PUMPKIN PATCH, AND...WELL, HE... HE'S.....WELL, HE'S...

OH, FORGET IT!

YOU'RE MORE TROUBLE THAN YOU'RE WORTH!

RATS!

NEW YEAR'S DAY AND WHERE AM I? ALONE IN A STRANGE COUNTRY.. WHAT IRONY!

HOW MUCH LONGER CAN THIS WAR GO ON? IF IT DOESN'T END SOON, I THINK I SHALL GO MAD!

GARÇON, ANOTHER ROOT BEER, PLEASE

HOW MANY ROOT BEERS CAN A MAN DRINK? HOW MANY DOES IT TAKE TO DRIVE THE AGONY FROM YOUR BRAIN? CURSE THIS WAR! CURSE THE MUD AND THE RAIN!

HERE'S THE WORLD WAR I FLYING ACE WALKING ONTO THE FIELD.."GOOD MORNING, CHAPS!" (THESE ARE GOOD LADS)

BUT WHAT'S THIS? THERE'S EXCITEMENT AMONG THE ENLISTED MEN... SOME SORT OF RUMOR GOING ABOUT..

HERE'S THE FLYING ACE REPORTING TO HIS COMMANDING OFFICER... "GOOD MORNING, SIR...A ROOT BEER? YES, SIR, I DON'T MIND IF I DO"

THERE MUST BE SOMETHING BIG COMING UP... HE ONLY OFFERS ME A ROOT BEER WHEN THERE'S A DANGEROUS MISSION TO BE FLOWN!

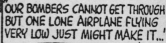

HERE'S THE WORLD WAR I FLYING ACE BEING AWAKENED TO FLY ANOTHER DAWN PATROL...

HERE'S THE WORLD WAR I FLYING ACE WALKING OUT ONTO THE FIELD...

IT SNOWED LAST NIGHT... BUT TODAY THE SUN IS OUT..THE SKY IS CLEAR...

I CLIMB INTO THE COCKPIT OF MY SOPWITH CAMEL...

"CHOCKS AWAY"

HERE'S THE WORLD WAR I FLYING ACE ZOOMING THROUGH THE AIR SEARCHING FOR THE RED BARON!

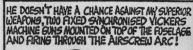

HE DOESN'T HAVE A CHANCE AGAINST MY SUPERIOR WEAPONS, TWO FIXED SYNCHRONISED VICKERS MACHINE GUNS MOUNTED ON TOP OF THE FUSELAGE AND FIRING THROUGH THE AIRSCREW ARC!

POW!

YOU'RE A POOR SPORT, RED BARON

SCHULZ

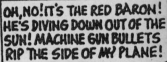

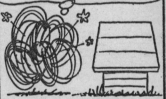

THEY'RE RIGHT...
IT IS A LONG WAY
TO TIPPERARY!

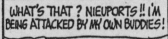

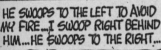

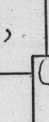

AH! HE HIT IT RIGHT TO MY SHORTSTOP! THIS'LL BE AN EASY OUT...

HERE'S THE WORLD WAR I FLYING ACE ZOOMING THROUGH THE AIR IN HIS SOPWITH CAMEL..

✳ SIGH ✳

NOW Peanuts Jewelry

Each item is 14 Kt. gold finish, hand-crafted cloisonné in brilliant colors, exquisitely designed by Aviva. Items shown in actual size. Complete satisfaction guaranteed or money refunded.

No. 10 pin $3

No. 11 pin $3

No. 12 pin $3

No. 13A pierced $3
No. 13B non-pierced $3

No. 14 pin $3

No. 15 pin $3

No. 16 pin $3

No. 17A pierced $3
No. 17B non-pierced $3

No. 18 pin $3

No. 19 pin $3

No. 20 pin $3

© United Feature Syndicate, Inc. 1971

No. 21 pin $3

No. 22 tie tack $3

No. 23 tie tack $3

No. 24 key chain $3

No. 25 money clip $4

No. 26 tie tack $3

No. 27 tie bar $3

No. 28 cufflinks $4

No. 29 pin $3

Please specify identity number of each item ordered and add 25¢ for each item to cover postage and handling. Personal check or money order. No cash. Send orders to HAMILTON HOUSE, Cos Cob, Conn. 06807.